EDGE BOOKS

MONSTER HANDBOOKS

WEREWOLVES

The Truth Behind
HISTORY'S SCARIEST SHAPE-SHIFTERS

by Sean McCollum

raintree 🍃

a Capstone company — publishers for children

Raintree is an imprint of Capstone Global Library Limited, a company incorporated in England and Wales having its registered office at 264 Banbury Road, Oxford, OX2 7DY – Registered company number: 6695582

www.raintree.co.uk
myorders@raintree.co.uk

Edited by Aaron Sautter
Designed by Bobbie Nuytten
Picture research by Gina Kammer
Production by Laura Manthe
Printed and bound in China.

ISBN 978 1 4747 0447 2 (hardcover)
19 18 17 16 15
10 9 8 7 6 5 4 3 2 1

ISBN 978 1 4747 0452 6 (paperback)
20 19 18 17 16
10 9 8 7 6 5 4 3 2 1

British Library Cataloguing in Publication Data

A full catalogue record for this book is available from the British Library.

Acknowledgements
Alamy: © Ivy Close Images, 11, © Jeff Morgan 10, 8, © Lordprice Collection, 23, © Pictorial Press Ltd, 25; Corbis: © Bettmann, 24; Dreamstime: © Mccool, (bottom) 21; Getty Images: De Agostini Picture Library, 14, Syfy, 28; Glow Images: Heritage Images/Ann Ronan Pictures, 19; Granger, NYC, (top) 17; Mary Evans Picture Library, 7; Newscom: akg-images, 12, Album/AMERICAN INTERNATIONAL PICTURES, 26; Shutterstock: andreiuc88, cover, 1, ARTEMENKO VALENTYN, 18, breaker213, 5, Brianito, 10, 30, Debbie Steinhausser, (bottom) 27, Larysa Ray, 4, Lasha Kilasonia, (Earth map) 9, Michael Vigliotti, (bottom) 17, Michal Jurkowski, (middle) 21, Nyord, cover, 1, Richard Peterson, (top) 21, SeDmi, 20, Shukaylova Zinaida, 13

Design Elements
Shutterstock: Ensuper (grunge background), Larysa Ray (grunge frames), Slava Gerj (grunge scratched background)

We would like to thank David Gilmore, Professor of Anthropology at Stony Brook University, New York, for his invaluable help in the preparation of this book.

Contents

POWER OF THE WOLF

As a full moon rises above the forest, fog creeps between the black shapes of the trees. Soon an eerie howl rises above the mist. "Ah-WOO-oooo!" When we hear that sound in a film it can mean only one thing – a werewolf is on the prowl!

Werewolves aren't real, but long ago many people believed they were. Wherever wolves have roamed, tales about werewolves have existed for thousands of years. The image of these fierce monsters has gone through many changes throughout history. Beliefs about werewolves in ancient times were very different from ideas held about them today.

In the past, these monsters often appeared as bloodthirsty predators. They prowled through the night and attacked anything that moved. But in modern stories werewolves are often the unfortunate victims of a **curse**. Sometimes they're even seen as heroes who fight to protect humans. But no matter how werewolves are portrayed, these **shape-shifters** have long had a powerful grip on people's imaginations.

curse evil spell meant to harm or punish someone
shape-shifter creature that is able to change its physical form

Chapter 1
SHAPE-SHIFTERS FROM LONG AGO

People have long been fascinated by the idea of humans changing into other creatures. Thousands of years ago ancient cultures often created tales featuring such shape-shifters.

Shape-shifters in ancient Greece

Shape-shifting was a common theme in stories from ancient Greece. Greek poets often told fantastic tales featuring half-human creatures such as mermaids and **centaurs**. Many ancient Greek stories also tell of how the gods changed people into dogs, deer, birds and other creatures.

The idea of people changing form wasn't limited to ancient Greek poets. The famous Greek historian Herodotus also passed along a story about shape-shifters. During his travels, Herodotus learned about the distant Neuri tribe. He was told that the Neuri people could turn into wolves once every year. Although Herodotus recorded this legend in his writings, he didn't believe the story himself.

centaur creature with the head and chest of a human and the body of a horse

FACT: In one ancient Greek tale, King Lycaon nearly tricks Zeus, the king of the gods, into eating human flesh. When Zeus learns about Lycaon's trick, he punishes the wicked king by turning him into a wolf.

Rome's wolf warriors

Rome was famous for its powerful army, which included specially trained "wolf" warriors. These soldiers wore the skins and skulls of wolves in order to "become the wolf" during battle. The Romans didn't believe these soldiers actually became wolves. But the **ritual** was thought to give them wolf-like strength and **cunning** in battle.

When Roman armies invaded central and northern Europe between 58 and 53 BC, they had a surprise waiting for them. They met Germanic people who also had fierce wolf-skin warriors. Reports state that these men were especially ferocious in battle. The Romans were impressed by these warriors. They even employed some of them to fight for Rome!

ritual   ceremony involving a set of religious actions

cunning   being sneaky or clever at tricking people

FACT: One Roman legend tells of two brothers, Romulus and Remus, who were raised by a wolf. The young men supposedly had wolf-like qualities such as cleverness, boldness and "wolf spirit". These mythical leaders are remembered as the founders of the great city of Rome.

Ancient cultures believed in a variety of shape-shifting creatures. Religious leaders and healers, known as shamans, were often thought to magically become other creatures. People believed that some shamans could even send their spirits into animals to control them.

NAVAJO PEOPLE
North America
shamans who turned into coyotes, wolves, owls and other animals

AMHARAN PEOPLE
Africa
hyena-people

JAPANESE
Asia
powerful fox spirits that could turn into people

AMAZON TRIBES
South America
stingray-men, snake-men

HAWAIIANS
Polynesia
shark-men

AZTECS
South America
jaguar-men

BALINESE
Indonesia
evil humans called layaks that could take the form of animals

Chapter 2
THE WEREWOLVES OF EUROPE

About 1,200 years ago, bands of Viking raiders swept across the British Isles and northern Europe. These warriors were reportedly so ferocious that people called them "wolves". Some of them even wore wolfskins and wolf heads. Soon a new name was whispered among their victims – "werewolf". It meant "man-wolf" or "outlaw-wolf" and described a person who could become a fierce killer.

FACT: Some stories from the 1500s described people who didn't actually turn into wolves. They looked normal, but were said to have the strength and vicious nature of a wolf.

Werewolves in the middle ages

During the Middle Ages (c. AD 500 to 1450), poems and tales about werewolves often appeared across Europe. These **medieval** stories sometimes showed werewolves as rational and gentle, or even as heroes. The heroic creatures were often people who had been cursed to become wolf-like creatures, but still tried to help others. In most tales, however, werewolves were terrifying monsters. They were violent beasts that often attacked and killed innocent people.

medieval having to do with the period of history between AD 500 and 1450

In the tale "William of Palermo," a friendly werewolf carries a young prince into the forest to protect him from his wicked uncle.

Becoming a werewolf

Medieval **folklore** shows a wide range of beliefs about how someone could become a werewolf. In some tales, people could change their form by magic. They may cast a spell, drink a magic potion or use a magical object to become a werewolf. German **peasants** often believed someone could put on a wolfskin belt and say some magic words to become a wolf.

In several medieval tales people make a deal with the Devil. These people sell their souls to receive the speed, strength and violent nature of a wolf.

In Serbia it was said that drinking rainwater from a wolf's footprint could turn someone into a werewolf. And in southern France, a few people were thought to have an uncontrollable urge to jump into a pond during a full moon. The person then climbed out of the water in the form of a wolf.

folkllore traditional knowledge and beliefs about a subject

peasant historical name for a poor and uneducated person who works on a farm

FACT: The idea that werewolves changed form during a full moon was first written about in the 1200s. But this didn't become a popular part of werewolf folklore until the early 1900s.

Werewolves on trial

During the Middle Ages people across Europe were very afraid of the **supernatural**. Books and pamphlets described many stories about monsters that harmed the innocent. These stories often caused people in towns and villages to panic. They sometimes jumped to conclusions about suspected werewolves – often with tragic results.

If a farmer found one of his animals had been killed violently, for example, he might suspect a wolf. But if no wolf was caught, he and others might think the killer was a werewolf instead. The hunt would soon be on for someone to blame. Perhaps a wandering stranger, or a person with a mental illness, would be accused of being a werewolf.

In France, Germany and other parts of Europe, mobs were sometimes formed to hunt down werewolves. When the suspects were captured, they were put on trial. These innocent people were often tortured until they confessed to being a werewolf. Then they were usually put to death.

supernatural something that cannot be given an ordinary explanation

THE WEREWOLF OF BEDBURG

In the 1580s the German village of Bedburg experienced several unexplained killings. Cattle were torn apart as though a vicious animal had attacked them. Then villagers began disappearing and were later found dead.

The villagers believed that a bloodthirsty wolf was on the prowl. They organized a hunt with dogs, and chased a wolf until they had it cornered. The hunters said they saw the wolf change into a local farmer called Peter Stubbe. Stubbe was put on trial as a werewolf and was found guilty. His wife and daughter were also found guilty of helping him. All three were put to death.

Chapter 3
DEFENCE AGAINST WEREWOLVES

At one time, tracking down a werewolf was like hunting any other animal. Werewolf hunters didn't use weapons believed to have magical powers. They instead used normal weapons such as swords, bows and arrows to hunt and kill werewolves.

The wolf of Ansbach

One such werewolf hunt took place in Germany in 1685. A wolf near the town of Ansbach had killed several farm animals. It had also reportedly attacked women and children. Rumours soon spread that the wolf was really the town's dead mayor. Some people thought that he had come back to life as a werewolf.

Armed with dogs, pitchforks and clubs, some local hunters trapped the wolf in a well and killed it. But the dead wolf didn't return to human form. To save their reputation, the hunters decided to make the wolf look like a real werewolf. They cut off its **muzzle** and put a mask over its face. They also put a wig on its head and dressed it in human clothes. They then hung the wolf in the town square to show everyone that they had killed a werewolf.

muzzle animal's nose, mouth and jaws

Waarhafftige Begebenheit!
Mit einem Verbannten Wolff: welcher im 1685ten Jahr im Margrafthum Onolzbach etliche Kinder weggetragen und gefressen. letzlich den 5 October in einen brunnen zu Neuses bey Eschen badtgefangen undt getödet. so dann dieser figur nach. aufgehängen Werden.

This gruesome tale shows how people once believed that werewolves could be killed with ordinary weapons. But this belief didn't last. In stories and myths about werewolves, killing them soon became much harder.

FACT: Wolves in England had been hunted to extinction by the end of the 1600s. As a result, werewolf tales in England were rare.

Changing the shape-shifter

By the 1800s werewolves in many stories were becoming scarier and more dangerous. People began to believe that magic was the best defence against these mythical beasts.

Many people thought magic could turn werewolves back into human beings. One method involved calling out a werewolf's human name three times. This supposedly forced the creature to immediately return to its human form.

Farmers in Germany claimed that iron and steel had a magical effect on werewolves. Throwing an iron or steel object over one of these monsters was thought to force it to become human again. The person's eyes were said to glow like a wolf's for a while afterwards.

In many stories, a werewolf's wife or husband had the ability to stop or reverse its transformation. One German tale tells of a farmer who saw a red-haired werewolf running through a field. He shouted out his wife's name and she transformed immediately.

Another story from Denmark describes a man who knew he would soon turn into a werewolf. He told his wife that if any animal attacked her, she should use her apron to defend herself. Before long a wolf appeared and the woman hit it with her apron. The wolf bit off a piece of the apron and ran away. Soon her husband returned with the piece of apron in his mouth. The man told his wife that he had been a werewolf. But she had helped break the curse and he was now just a normal man again.

Some old tales described "wolf charmers" as people who used musical magic spells to control both ordinary wolves and werewolves.

monkshood,
also known
as wolfsbane

Magical werewolf weapons

In many tales, werewolves couldn't
be cured or turned back into humans.
The monsters instead had to be killed.
By the 1800s, however, werewolves in
most stories had grown very powerful.
Ordinary weapons, such as pitchforks and
arrows, could no longer pierce their hides.
And normal bullets just bounced off of
them. Sharp-edged weapons, such as axes
or swords, might work – but only if they
were made of iron.

To solve this problem, werewolf folklore
began to include magical weapons that
could kill the beasts. In some parts of
Europe, plants with magical properties
were said to be the best weapons. A stake
from alder wood could pierce a werewolf's
magical hide and kill it. The poisonous
flower known as **wolfsbane** was also
thought to be an effective werewolf weapon.

wolfsbane   poisonous plant with
purple hood–like flowers

People in Germany thought that **inherited** silver could harm werewolves. For example, a bullet made from an inherited silver button could kill or wound a werewolf. People could also use a parent's silver dagger or knife to kill these monsters.

inherit to receive someone's property after they die

alder wood stake

silver bullet

silver dagger

Chapter 4
WILD ABOUT WEREWOLVES

A pair of hikers walk along a dark and secluded forest path. Suddenly they hear a wolf's howl. They run away, but just when they think they're safe, the werewolf attacks! Then somewhere in the darkened cinema, a terrified person screams.

Many people enjoy being frightened by monsters and scary stories. Since the 1900s few scary creatures have been more popular than werewolves. Rather than being half-forgotten characters in old folk tales, werewolves became superstars of fiction.

Werewolf literature

In the mid-1800s, the image of the werewolf began to change. Writers took the old tales about the monsters and turned them into stories that everybody could enjoy. Stories featuring werewolves, vampires and other monsters soon became best-sellers. *The Man-Wolf* (1831), "A Story of a Weir-Wolf" (1846) and *Wagner, the Wehr-Wolf* (1846) are just a few examples.

By the end of the 1800s, werewolf tales were more popular than ever. People enjoyed reading the thrills and chills of how werewolves were created, and how to fight them. But the invention of film would cause their popularity to explode.

The Book of Were-Wolves *by Sabine Baring-Gould was first published in 1865. It is filled with folk tales and illustrations of werewolves.*

Werewolves go to Hollywood

Werewolves got their big break in films during the mid-1900s. Hollywood released one of its first werewolf films, *Werewolf of London*, in 1935. But in 1941 *The Wolf Man* really got audiences shrieking.

People loved it. They finally got to see just how exciting and scary werewolves could be. Two years later, werewolves thrilled people again in the film *Frankenstein Meets the Wolf Man*.

Hollywood films changed many of the rules for werewolves. In the past, werewolves had often been people who chose to become monsters. Hunting and killing them was also fairly simple. But Hollywood's new rules made werewolves more terrifying. They had supernatural strength and speed. And they were difficult to kill. Ordinary bullets and other non-magical weapons could not harm them.

FACT: For *The Wolf Man* (1941), actor Lon Chaney Jr sat still for nine hours while artists put on his make-up.

In the mid-1900s, Hollywood established several new rules for werewolves in films. Some of these include:

➤ werewolves change shape under the light of a full moon

➤ werewolves walk on two legs like humans

➤ werewolves have supernatural strength and speed, and are not harmed by ordinary bullets or weapons

➤ in human form, werewolves can be good people, but they usually become violent killers in werewolf form

➤ a victim who is bitten or scratched by a werewolf will later become a werewolf

➤ wolfsbane can weaken or even kill werewolves

➤ weapons made of silver, such as bullets and knives, can injure or kill werewolves

The film I Was a Teenage Werewolf *was a big hit with audiences in 1957.*

The popular werewolf

The popularity of *The Wolf Man* revealed how much people enjoyed being scared by these make-believe monsters. The popularity of werewolves continued to climb. During the 1950s, several more films were made featuring everyone's favourite wild monsters. Werewolves were soon seen everywhere, from films and comic books, to children's toys and TV programmes. Werewolves were also a popular costume choice at Halloween. People wore werewolf masks, furry gloves with plastic claws and plastic werewolf fangs.

Werewolves shift again

In the 1980s and 1990s, werewolves became easier to like. In several stories they were shown as victims of a terrible curse. Werewolves even became heroes in some stories. They resisted the urge to kill, and tried to avoid people when in wolf form.

This shift in the image of werewolves in popular culture may have reflected changes in people's feelings about real wolves. People feared and hated wild wolves for hundreds of years. But in the 1970s people became more aware of wolves' important role in nature. When wolves nearly became extinct in much of North America, it was decided to include them in the US Endangered Species Act. This 1973 law states that endangered animals can't be hunted or killed by humans.

Today in North America, wolf populations have bounced back. Thousands of wolves roam in the wild.

Werewolves of today and tomorrow

Today, werewolves appear in almost every form of entertainment. Ideas about these creatures have changed throughout history, and continue to evolve today. In many recent stories, wolf-men and wolf-women can transform whenever they wish – no full moon is required. Sometimes they become four-footed creatures, as in the *Twilight* books and films. In other stories they may change into a human-wolf **hybrid**. In certain stories, people also no longer need to be bitten by a werewolf to become one. Sometimes these creatures are born into werewolf families or "packs". Being a werewolf is just a part of who they are.

Whether they have new abilities, or use their strength to protect the innocent, werewolves continue to surprise audiences. In this way they remain true to werewolf legends of ancient days. These popular monsters are constantly shifting, in their character as well as their shape.

hybrid plant or animal that has traits from two different species

Transforming into a werewolf is often shown to be very painful in modern films and TV series.

WEREWOLVES IN FILMS, TV AND BOOKS

TITLE	MEDIA	CHARACTER	GOOD OR BAD
Werewolf of London (1935)	film	Wilfred Glendon	good person / bad wolf
The Wolf Man (1941)	film	Larry Talbot	good person / bad wolf
I Was a Teenage Werewolf (1957)	film	Tony Rivers	good person / bad wolf
The Curse of the Werewolf (1961)	film	Leon Corledo	good person / bad wolf
Teen Wolf (1985)	film	Scott Howard	good person/good wolf
The Monster Squad (1987)	film	Wolfman	good person / bad wolf
Buffy the Vampire Slayer (1997–2003)	TV	Daniel "Oz" Osbourne	good person / bad wolf
Harry Potter series (1997–2007)	novels	Fenrir Greyback Remus Lupin	bad person / bad wolf good person / bad wolf
Twilight series (2005–2008)	novels	Jacob Black	good person / good wolf
The Boy Who Cried Werewolf (2010)	TV movie	Jordan Sands	good person / good wolf
Grimm (2011–present)	TV	Monroe	good person / good wolf

GLOSSARY

centaur creature with the head and chest of a human and the body of a horse

cunning being sneaky or clever at tricking people

curse evil spell meant to harm or punish someone

folklore traditional knowledge and beliefs about a subject

hybrid plant or animal that has traits from two different species

inherit to receive someone's property after they die

medieval having to do with the period of history between AD 500 and 1450

muzzle animal's nose, mouth and jaws

peasant historical name for a poor and uneducated person who works on a farm

ritual ceremony involving a set of religious actions

shape-shifter creature that is able to change its physical form

supernatural something that cannot be given an ordinary explanation

wolfsbane poisonous plant with purple hood-like flowers

BOOKS

The Werewolf Hunter's Guide (Monster Tracker),
Ursula Lestrade (Franklin Watts, 2011)

Vampires and Werewolves (Solving Mysteries with Science),
Jane Bingham (Raintree, 2014)

Vampires vs Werewolves: Battle of the Bloodthirsty Beasts
(Monster Wars), Michael O'Hearn (Raintree, 2012)

WEBSITES

www.crystalinks.com/werewolves.html
Read more about the history of werewolves from ancient
times to today.

www.joteel.com/werewolf/index.htm
Discover more about werewolves in ancient mythology,
medieval lore, and explanations for werewolf beliefs.

www.mythicalcreaturesguide.com/page/Werewolf
Learn more about werewolves and folklore from around
the world.

INDEX